Camaros

ERIC ETHAN

Gareth Stevens Publishing
MILWAUKEE

For a free color catalog describing Gareth Stevens Publishing's list of high-quality books and multimedia programs, call 1-800-542-2595 (USA) or 1-800-461-9120 (Canada). Gareth Stevens Publishing's Fax: (414) 225-0377. See our catalog, too, on the World Wide Web: http://gsinc.com

Library of Congress Cataloging-in-Publication Data

Ethan, Eric.
      Camaros / by Eric Ethan.
            p. cm. — (Great American muscle cars—an imagination
      library series.
      Includes index.
      Summary: Surveys the history of the Chevrolet Camaro and its
      designs, engines, performance, and costs.
        ISBN 0-8368-1742-7 (lib. bdg.)
        1. Camaro automobile—Juvenile literature.   [1. Camaro automobile.]
      I. Title. II. Series: Ethan, Eric. Great American muscle cars—an
      imagination library series.
      TL215.C33E84   1998
      629.222'2—dc21   97-31771

First published in North America in 1998 by
Gareth Stevens Publishing
1555 North RiverCenter Drive, Suite 201
Milwaukee, WI 53212 USA

This edition © 1998 by Gareth Stevens, Inc. Text by Eric Ethan. Photographs by Nicky Wright (pages 5, 7, and 9), Ron Kimball (cover, pages 15, 17, 19, and 21), and John Lamm (pages 11 and 13). Additional end matter © 1998 by Gareth Stevens, Inc.

Text: Eric Ethan
Page layout: Eric Ethan, Helene Feider
Cover design: Helene Feider
Series design: Shari Tikus

Printed in the United States of America

1 2 3 4 5 6 7 8 9 02 01 00 99 98

TABLE OF CONTENTS

Words that appear in the glossary are printed in **boldface** type the first time they occur in the text.

THE FIRST CAMAROS

Camaros are made by Chevrolet, a division of General Motors, in Detroit, Michigan. The first Camaros were built in late 1966. Many people thought Chevrolet was trying to copy the popular Ford Mustang.

But the Camaro was built to replace another Chevrolet car called the Corvair. Corvairs were mid-engined cars that could be ordered with bucket seats, faster motors, and other sports car **options**. The Corvair had a reputation for being a dangerous car. Chevrolet stopped making Corvairs in 1965. In 1966, it **designed** the Camaro to take its place.

*Muscle cars, like the Camaro, are American-made, two-door sports **coupes** with powerful engines made for high-performance driving. Camaros, like this 1967 slate blue hardtop, have special Super Sport high-performance options.*

WHAT DO CAMAROS LOOK LIKE?

Camaros do look a little like Mustangs. Both have long hoods and short rear decks. These were common features of a type of automobile called a Pony car. The Pontiac Firebird and Plymouth Barracuda are other examples of Pony cars.

The Camaro had round lines over the wheels and sides of the passenger **compartment** to make it look like European sports cars of the era. The 1968 Camaro pictured came with the Super Sport option package. Toward the front bumper, you can see the SS logo. Camaros with the Super Sport package had special speed equipment like a **spoiler**. When a car is going fast, a spoiler pushes the car down toward the road for safer handling.

This 1968 Chevrolet Camaro SS has the long hood and short rear deck styling common to Pony cars.

WHAT WAS THE FASTEST CAMARO?

Basic Camaros came from the factory with a 250-cubic-inch (4.1-liter) engine. The greater the cubic inches, the faster the car. People wanting even more power could order a 396-cubic-inch (6.5-liter) engine that produced 375 **horsepower**.

The fastest Camaro was the Z-28 built in 1967 and 1968. Z-28s were packed with special equipment like **disc** brakes and **air dams**. Speedometers on Z-28s indicated speeds up to 120 miles (195 kilometers) per hour. But, in fact, Z-28s could go nearly 150 miles (240 km) per hour. Few Z-28s were built for the public. Chevrolet was concerned about driver safety in this car. Most Z-28s were sold for professional racing.

Modified Camaros like the car pictured had larger engines and special exhaust pipes. They could easily exceed 120 miles (195 km) per hour.

CAMARO ENGINES

Chevrolet offered several different engines for the Camaro. The small 6-cylinder provided good gas mileage but was not very fast. Larger V8 engines made for a much faster car. Special speed equipment could also be added to the engines.

The most powerful engine available to Camaro customers at the time was a standard 427-cubic-inch (7-liter) engine modified to produce 450 horsepower. One important modification to this engine was the **air cleaner**. It was open all around the top to allow the maximum amount of air to flow through. More air equals more power in high-performance engines.

A 1969 Yenko modified Z-28 Camaro engine. Yenko, an auto dealership, worked closely with Chevrolet during the 1960s to produce high-performance versions of the Camaro.

3 1833 03128 2046

11

CAMARO INTERIORS

High-performance Camaros generally came with bucket seats like the ones pictured. On the headrest at the top of the seat, the letters *SYG* are visible. This indicates the car is a special Yenko-modified Camaro. Yenko-modified Camaros included special speed and handling equipment, which made the car faster and safer to drive at high speeds.

The special equipment included **gauges** located below the dashboard to the right of the **stick shift**.

The interior of a 1969 Yenko-modified Z-28 Camaro.

13

CAMAROS RACING

During the 1960s, Chevrolet was actively involved in road racing. Racing automobiles gave the company a chance to test new designs. When Chevrolet won races, the popularity of the cars increased. Z-28 models, specially created for road racing, won many races in 1967-1968. They contained very powerful engines with nearly 400 horsepower.

Some Camaros have been made into **drag racers** (dragsters). Drag racers race at top speed for a quarter mile. The cars race in a straight line only, so it does not matter how well a car corners. The Z-28 Camaro pictured has been made into a dragster. It has a special air intake on top of the motor to help the engine run faster.

This 1967 Chevy Camaro street rod has been heavily modified to compete in drag races.

BEAUTIFUL CAMAROS

The name *Camaro* was taken from a French word meaning "companion" or "pal." By 1969 when the ZL-1 model pictured was built, Camaro had a lot of pals. Almost 700,000 cars were sold from 1967 to 1970.

Only a few changes were made in the ZL-1 because the first design was so popular. It was a very fast car with a V-8 motor. A **hood scoop** is visible just ahead of the windshield.

Can you see the hood scoop just ahead of the windshield on this ZL-1?

THE LAST ORIGINAL CAMAROS

Muscle cars began to disappear in the 1970s. The price of gasoline was very high, and the big muscle car engines used a lot of it. Bigger engines also cause more air **pollution**, and people were concerned about the environment. But pollution equipment kept the muscle cars from reaching full power. Safety is important, too. Not everyone can drive a fast car safely.

Camaros are still made today. Over the last thirty years, Chevrolet **engineers** have worked hard to meet new safety and pollution standards.

Modern Camaros like this one built in 1994 look very different from those made in the 1960s.

WHAT DID CAMAROS COST?

Through the 1960s, Chevrolet kept the price of Camaros lower than most full-sized models. They were less expensive than their biggest **rival** — the Ford Mustang. It was hard to spend more than $4,000 on a Camaro. Even the Z-28 with all the racing options cost only $400 more than the basic model.

Chevrolet kept the Camaro reasonably priced because it used a **component** approach to its car line. Many Camaro parts were also used in the Chevy II and Chevelle models. This allowed Chevrolet to make large numbers of similar parts. This lowered overall cost.

Camaros with special Super Sport high-performance packages like the 1968 model pictured were just a little more expensive than standard models.

WHAT DO CAMAROS COST TODAY?

A surprising number of original Camaros have survived. Collectors work many hours to **restore** and maintain these classic muscle cars. Basic models in good condition with small engines and few options are worth more than the cars originally cost.

Rare models are worth many times their original price. Full-race Z-28s in restored condition are valued at over $30,000. The 1967 Z-28 is a very rare model. Only 602 were manufactured.

Even the more common Super Sport model, pictured on the previous page, is valued at many times its original purchase price.

GLOSSARY

air cleaner — The part of a car that filters the air before it enters the engine compartment.

air dam — A wall or other shape that holds back or guides air.

compartment (kom-PART-ment) — A separate area surrounded by four walls or sides.

component (kum-POH-nent) — An element or part of a whole.

coupe (koop) — An enclosed, two-door automobile that is normally smaller than a sedan.

design (dee-ZINE) — The plans and specifications for a new product.

disc (DISK) — A thin, flat, circular object.

drag racer (DRAG RASE-er) — A car that competes in an acceleration contest with other cars in a straight line.

engineer (ehn-jin-EER) — In the automobile industry, a person who designs and builds engines.

gauge (gayj) — An instrument that indicates how well or poorly a motor is operating.

hood scoop —The part of a car that brings fresh air into the engine compartment.

horsepower (HORS POW-er) — A system for measuring engine ability based on the amount of weight one horse can pull.

option (OP-shun) — A feature that can be added over and above the regular features.

pollution (poh-LU-shun) — Wastes and poisons that enter the air, land, and water.

restore (ree-STOR) — To fix an item so that it becomes like new.

rival (RYE-vel) — A competitor.

spoiler (SPOYL-er) — A small lip at the back of the trunk on an automobile. When a car is traveling fast, a spoiler will push the car down toward the road for safer handling.

stick shift (STIHK shift) — A manually operated gearshift that is mounted on the steering column or floor of an automobile.

WEB SITES

www.chevrolet.com

www.camaroz28.com/

www.camaroclub.com

www.camarosite.com

PLACES TO WRITE

Classic Motorbooks
729 Prospect Avenue, P.O. Box 1
Osceola, WI 54020 1-800-826-6600

U.S. Camaro Club
P.O. Box 608167
Orlando, FL 32860 1-407-880-1967

Pensacola Classic Chevy Club
P.O. Box 844
Shalimar, FL 32579

Los Angeles Classic Chevy Club
P.O. Box 45-1955
Los Angeles, CA 10045-1955

INDEX